Cupid
the Dolphin

Rob Waring, *Series Editor*

T0354109

HEINLE
CENGAGE Learning™

Australia • Brazil • Japan • Korea • Mexico • Singapore • Spain • United Kingdom • United States

Words to Know

This story is set in the United States. It begins in Galveston [gælvəstən], Texas, which is on the coast of the Gulf of Mexico, and ends in Vallejo [vəleɪhoʊ], California.

 A **Dolphins.** Read the paragraph. Then match each word or phrase with the correct definition.

Dolphins are mammals, just like humans. However, unlike humans, they are marine mammals, which means that they live in the sea. Dolphins are closely related to whales, but they are usually much smaller. There are almost 40 types of dolphin around the world, including the bottlenose dolphin. Even though dolphins are very intelligent animals, they can sometimes get stranded on the beach due to illness or injury.

1. mammal _____	**a.** unable to leave a place
	b. a very common type of dolphin
2. marine _____	**c.** related to the sea
3. whale _____	**d.** a warm-blooded animal which feeds its own milk to its young
4. bottlenose dolphin _____	**e.** a very large sea animal that breathes air through a hole on the top of its head
5. stranded _____	

bottlenose dolphins

B Dolphin Rescue.
Read the definitions. Then complete the paragraph with the correct form of the underlined words.

A predator is an animal that kills and eats other animals.

Rescue means to help someone or something out of a dangerous or unpleasant situation.

A stretcher is a piece of soft material between two long poles that is used to move people or animals that can't move by themselves.

Volunteers are people who work without being forced or paid to do so.

The Texas Marine Mammal Stranding Network is an organisation that (1) _____ ocean animals that are stranded on beaches. Many of its members are (2) _____ who work for the organisation for free. When a dolphin is saved, it is usually put on a (3) _____ and taken to a rescue centre to get better. If these dolphins are released into the sea again without help, they may die or be attacked by (4) _____.

stretcher

Volunteers Rescuing Stranded Dolphins

whale

When you see him happily swimming around, it's hard to think that Cupid is lucky to be alive. On February 14, 2003, this bottlenose dolphin was found stranded on a beach in Texas. **Tammy Renaud**[1] of the Texas Marine Mammal Stranding Network describes what Cupid was like when he was first found. 'When we first saw him on the beach, he was very **lethargic**,'[2] she explains. 'He just looked **pathetic**.[3] He was just a sad little dolphin lying on the beach needing help.'

---

[1]**Tammy Renaud:** [tæmi: rənoʊ]
[2]**lethargic:** having no energy; very tired
[3]**pathetic:** sad and helpless

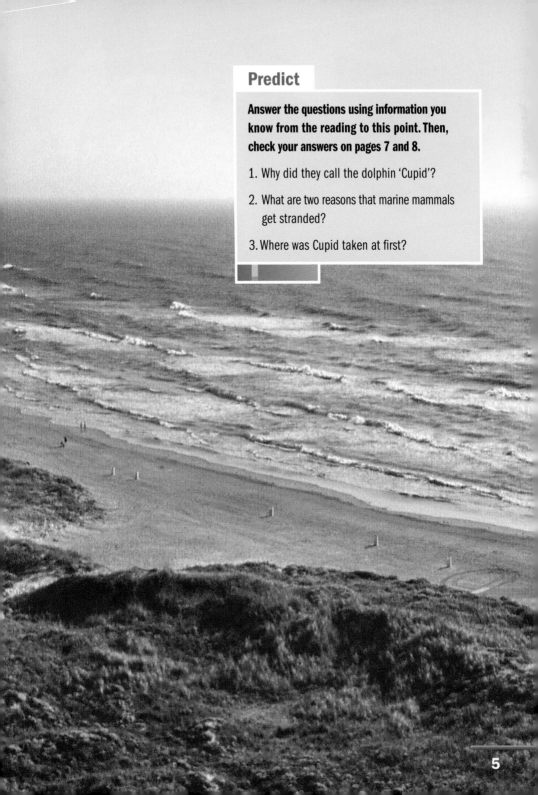

Predict

Answer the questions using information you know from the reading to this point. Then, check your answers on pages 7 and 8.

1. Why did they call the dolphin 'Cupid'?

2. What are two reasons that marine mammals get stranded?

3. Where was Cupid taken at first?

Nobody knows exactly how Cupid became stranded that **Valentine's Day**,[4] but it's not unusual for dolphins or whales to be found on beaches. Thousands of marine animals are stranded every year, and many of them don't survive. Renaud explains why these strandings occur. 'Strandings can happen due to illness, due to injury, due to a number of things,' she says.

A stranded whale or dolphin is in immediate danger and will usually die within days, sometimes even hours. If the animal is released directly back into the sea, it will probably die, get stranded again or be eaten by predators. However, if the animal stays on the beach without human help, it will certainly die as well.

---

[4]**Valentine's Day:** a U.S. holiday on February 14 when people express their love to others
NOTE: 'Cupid' is the name of the Roman god of love.

Cupid, however, was lucky. A fisherman called Christopher Cruse found him and called the Texas Marine Mammal Stranding Network. Renaud tells the story. 'We don't know how long Cupid had been there on the beach before Christopher found him. The speediness of [Christopher's] actions saved Cupid.' Renaud then explains that Christopher really helped Cupid by keeping people away from the injured animal and by keeping Cupid calm. The volunteers from Renaud's organisation rushed to the beach to examine Cupid and assess his condition. They knew that they had to get him to the rescue centre pool as fast as possible.

The time period when a dolphin is out of the sea is extremely important. Keeping the animal wet is essential; if it doesn't stay wet enough, it could die. In Cupid's case, the rescue volunteers did a great job. They carefully placed him on a stretcher and loaded him in a borrowed lorry. Then, they kept him safe and wet until they were able to get him to their rescue centre pool.

The Texas Marine Mammal Stranding Network, has been carefully watching 1,000 **miles**[5] of Texas coast for more than 25 years. The organisation doesn't have a lot of money to keep large sea mammals alive. They simply couldn't manage it without the 2,000 volunteers who give their time and energy to help. Why do the volunteers do it? They do it purely for their love of sea creatures, like Cupid.

Renaud says that the people who work in the network are very close. 'I equate this to being one big family,' she explains. 'A lot of people take care of each other around here, they take care of the animals, and it's just a really **neat**[6] thing to be a part of.'

---

[5]**mile:** 1 mile = 1.61 kilometres
[6]**neat:** *(slang)* great; wonderful

More than 90 per cent of the mammals that are rescued by the Network are bottlenose dolphins, like Cupid. Once these animals are transferred to the rescue centre, more volunteers get involved. With Cupid, a team of volunteers closely observed him for the first few days. 'The first 72 hours are what we call our **"critical care"**[7] period,' says Renaud. Anything could happen to a weakened animal during this time. If the animal survives this critical care period, then there is a better chance that it will live.

Several volunteers came to help Cupid through the dangerous time after his arrival. In fact, they were practically lining up to watch over the pathetic little dolphin! There were even plenty of volunteers who offered to get up early and work between 4 a.m. and 8 a.m., which is not a popular time to help. The volunteers worked every hour of the day and night. They stood with Cupid in his pool, walked him around in the water and held him in their arms. Everyone really wanted the poor, lethargic animal to survive, but no one knew for sure if he would or not.

---

[7]**critical care:** the specialised care of injuries that are life-threatening

During Cupid's time in the rescue centre, volunteers noticed something unusual about the dolphin. At the time, Renaud talked about the unusual actions: 'When he's not sleeping, he looks like every other dolphin; it's just when he's resting that he has these abnormal periods. He swims in tight circles. Sometimes he swims **belly-up**.[8] He swims on his side a lot.' These are all very unusual behavioural characteristics for dolphins. Eventually the team at the rescue centre found the cause: Cupid suffers from an illness that is similar to human **epilepsy**![9]

---

[8]**belly-up:** on one's back; with the stomach or 'belly' turned upwards
[9]**epilepsy:** an illness affecting the nervous system that causes uncontrolled movements and sometimes loss of awareness

Sequence the Events

What is the correct order of the events? Write numbers.

_____ Renaud and the team brought Cupid back to the centre in a lorry.

_____ Christopher called the Texas Marine Mammal Stranding Network.

_____ Christopher found Cupid stranded on the beach.

_____ Cupid started to get better.

_____ A team of volunteers watched over Cupid carefully.

According to Renaud, everyone at the centre was very worried about Cupid; especially when he had these **episodes**[10] of illness. She says, 'Our concern was that if we [were to] put him back in the wild, would he be able to protect himself if he was in one of those episodes? We couldn't answer that for sure.' So, the team began a long process of treatment and tests to help them understand Cupid's problem.

Renaud reports how Cupid's illness makes him different from other dolphins. 'He should be able to shut down half of his brain when he sleeps, and maintain enough **consciousness**[11] to breathe. [He should be able] to come to the surface [and] to be aware of what's going on around him,' she explains. Because he can't do these things, Cupid could easily get into trouble if he was released back out in the sea.

---

[10]**episode:** one in a series of events
[11]**consciousness:** awareness; ability to think and notice things

Over the next few weeks, the volunteers helped with weekly blood tests and examinations to check Cupid's health. They also worked to find out why he stranded himself in the first place. The volunteers really loved and cared for Cupid. With this special care, his individual character grew and grew. At first he was scared, but then he became playful under their care. Like any youngster, the dolphin loved his toys and playing in the pool. These are all good signs for a dolphin!

As Cupid grew happier, he also grew healthier – and fatter! By the end of his stay at the centre, he was 62 **pounds**[12] heavier and two and a half **inches**[13] longer than when he arrived. Of course, he was always hungry too; he was eating 11 pounds of fish every day!

[12]**pound:** 1 pound = 0.45 kilograms
[13]**inch:** 1 inch = 2.54 centimetres

It was unusual for a rescued dolphin to spend this much time at the centre in Galveston, but finding a new home for Cupid was becoming very difficult. The weeks turned into months. Everyone at the centre really liked the friendly dolphin, and didn't want to see him go – but they knew he couldn't stay.

Renaud and the team had to make a very hard decision: What should they do with Cupid? If they released him back into the sea, he would die because of his illness. However, they just didn't have the resources to look after a fast-growing dolphin. Finally, in early 2004, Vallejo, California's Marine World agreed to take Cupid.

Identify Cause and Effect

Circle the cause and underline the effect in each of the sentences.

1. Cupid's individual character grew as the volunteers loved and cared for him.

2. If they put Cupid back in the sea, he would die.

3. The dolphin became fatter when he became happier.

At first, the people at Marine World California were concerned about Cupid getting sick. They decided to keep him away from other dolphins for his own health and safety. While he became familiar with his new environment, the other dolphins at Marine World practised nearby for a performance. The dolphins at Marine World California are trained to do a number of tricks. They can jump high out of the water and they also try to 'speak' with their trainers. When they do these things, they often receive a special treat – fish!

Not everyone agrees that teaching animals how to perform is a good idea. There is some controversy, or disagreement, about the subject. Dan Cartwright was one of the trainers who worked with Cupid when he first arrived. At the time, he talked about this issue. 'That's always a controversy ... keeping any animal **in captivity**,'[14] he says, 'but I hope people understand that we're doing something good here. This animal cannot be released again, but he's going to have a nice life here. We take very good care of the animals; [we do] nothing but the best for them.'

---

[14]**in captivity:** unable to move and act freely; kept within a limited area

The people at Marine World were really excited to introduce Cupid to the other dolphins. The truth is, dolphins are very social animals and they love to communicate with other dolphins. They seem to have a special relationship with humans as well. According to Cartwright: 'It's something special. Everywhere you go, everybody loves a dolphin.' He then adds, 'I've heard stories from Spanish guys that were in the war that were on a **downed**[15] plane or downed boat. [They were] telling me stories of dolphins actually circling them to protect them. I believe it … I completely believe it! I've never seen it with my own eyes, but I absolutely believe it.'

Many people believe that there is something really magical about dolphins. There are stories about their ability to recognise women who are going to have babies, or recognise illnesses in humans. Some people even say that dolphins can help sick people to get better. They also have highly developed communication skills. Scientists actually believe that dolphins have their own language of unusual sounds!

---

[15]**downed:** a downed plane or boat has been damaged and made to fall or sink

And as for Cupid? He was kept alone for 30 days, then the trainers were able to put him into the main dolphin pool. In total, he had lived alone for nearly a year. When he was released, the previously 'sad, little dolphin' was very excited to be with other dolphins again.

Nowadays, Cupid is settled in his new home and has a happy future ahead of him. He was lucky that he survived being stranded, and especially lucky that he met the wonderful volunteers at the Texas Marine Mammal Stranding Network. Without them, and all of their hard work, there probably wouldn't be a friendly dolphin named Cupid!

After You Read

1. On page 4, 'him' refers to a:
   A. Texas Marine Mammal Stranding Network member
   B. fish
   C. whale
   D. mammal

2. When Tammy Renaud first saw Cupid, she thought he was:
   A. pitiful
   B. fearless
   C. embarrassing
   D. lacking

3. Other animals might eat a stranded dolphin.
   A. True
   B. False

4. The word 'assess' on page 8 means:
   A. estimate
   B. evaluate
   C. energise
   D. extend

5. According to Tammy, what have the volunteers created?
   A. a disagreement
   B. an exchange
   C. a community
   D. a production

6. What's a good heading for the second paragraph on page 12?
   A. Scared Dolphin
   B. Swimming Together
   C. A Loving End
   D. Committed Volunteers

7. _____Cupid was in the rescue centre, the workers noticed something unusual.

    A. During

    B. While

    C. However

    D. If

8. What does Cupid lack when he sleeps?

    A. epilepsy

    B. dreams

    C. awareness

    D. air

9. What does the word 'signs' mean on page 18?

    A. indications

    B. symbols

    C. advertisements

    D. cases

10. The controversy discussed on page 23 is about whether dolphins should:

    A. eat fish

    B. be rescued

    C. jump and play

    D. learn to perform

11. Dan Cartwright believes that dolphins:

    A. like to play with planes

    B. don't like each other

    C. are caring creatures

    D. make people nervous

12. What's the usual goal of the Texas Marine Mammal Stranding Network?

    A. to release rescued dolphins back to the wild

    B. to send dolphins to Marine World

    C. to build a bond between people and dolphins

    D. to learn to communicate with other mammals

PROTECT OUR DOLPHINS AND WHALES!

Dolphins and whales are two of the world's favourite marine mammals. In the past 25 years, people all over the world have become interested in keeping these animals safe. Here are some ways people are helping:

LEGAL AID

In 1990, several laws were passed that required fishing boats to use methods that would not injure dolphins. Before this, mother dolphins were often separated from their babies when fishing boats chased them to find fish. Adult dolphins were also often caught in fishing nets. These animals would die because they couldn't get to the surface for air.

VOLUNTEER ORGANISATIONS

Today, many volunteer groups are working to protect the marine mammal populations around the world. The Ocean Conservation Society in Los Angeles, California, has started an 'Adopt-a-Dolphin' programme. The programme invites people to look at pictures of dolphins on their website. Site visitors can then provide financial support for their favourite dolphin. The animals actually remain in the wild, but the money is used to support dolphin research and rescue programmes. In Texas, another group of volunteers cleans up the beach at the Padre Island National Seashore on a regular basis. By removing rubbish, they're helping to create a safe environment for all marine life.

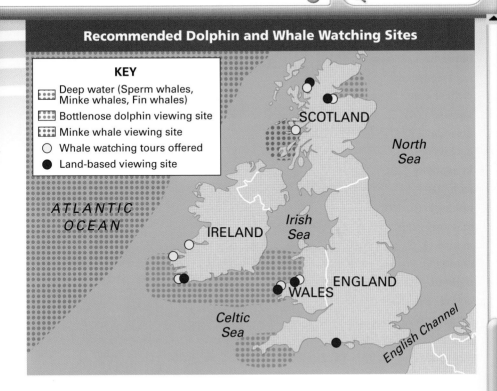

Recommended Dolphin and Whale Watching Sites

KEY

- Deep water (Sperm whales, Minke whales, Fin whales)
- Bottlenose dolphin viewing site
- Minke whale viewing site
- ○ Whale watching tours offered
- ● Land-based viewing site

SCOTLAND

North Sea

ATLANTIC OCEAN

IRELAND

Irish Sea

ENGLAND

WALES

Celtic Sea

English Channel

EDUCATIONAL PROGRAMMES

The Whale and Dolphin Conservation Society (WDCS) in the United Kingdom provides a number of educational programmes about dolphins. WDCS members develop educational materials and make frequent presentations at schools about protecting dolphins. In addition, the society supports dolphin-friendly programmes in other parts of the world, including South America and Asia. Their 'Out of the Blue' trips take people to places such as Greece and South Africa to see whales and dolphins in their natural settings. Closer to home, the WDCS provides maps to show people where to see whales and dolphins in their area. Land-based sites even allow viewers to watch from the coast rather than a boat. The WDCS encourages people to send in reports of sightings so that they can use the information in their research programmes.

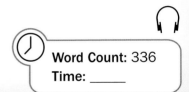

Word Count: 336
Time: _____

Vocabulary List

belly-up (14)
bottlenose dolphin (2, 4, 12)
consciousness (17)
critical care (12)
downed (24)
episode (17)
epilepsy (14)
in captivity (23)
inch (18)
lethargic (4, 12)
mammal (2, 3, 4, 5, 8, 11, 12, 15, 27)
marine (2, 3, 4, 5, 7, 8, 11, 15, 20, 23, 24, 27)
neat (11)
pathetic (4, 12)
pound (18)
predator (3, 7)
rescue (3, 8, 12, 14, 20)
stranded (2, 3, 4, 5, 7, 15, 18, 27)
stretcher (3, 8)
volunteer (3, 8, 11, 12, 14, 15, 18, 21, 27)
whale (2, 3, 7)